The Colour of British Rail Vol. 2

EAST COAST
— MAIN LINE —
1960 – 1992

GAVIN W. MORRISON

DESIGNED BY BARNABUS
TYPESET BY TYPESTYLE, TRURO, CORNWALL
PRINTED BY CENTURY LITHO, PENRYN, CORNWALL
BOUND BY BOOTHS BOOKBINDERS, PENRYN, CORNWALL

ISBN 0-906899-46-X

British Library Cataloguing in Publication Data
A catalogue reference for this book is available
from the British Library.

FRONT COVER:

ltic No. 55002 *The King's Own Yorkshire Light Infantry* was e one chosen by the National Railway Museum to resent the class in their collection. It was handed over at eremony in the museum on 12th December, 1980, after ng painted in the original green livery but with full yellow ds. It continued in service until 2nd January, 1982, when it s withdrawn in working order, and placed in the museum. s shown on one of the last regular Deltic diagrams heading e up 14-10 York-Kings Cross overtaking ex-works Class 47 47004, on the newly realigned track, alongside Doncaster pot on 16th April, 1981. – *Gavin Morrison.*

REAR COVER:

e evening shadows are falling as an HST on the 1600 gs Cross-Edinburgh glitters in the evening sunshine as it proaches Tweedmouth on 10th June, 1978. – *Gavin orrison.*

RIGHT:

e extremely complicated track work at Kings Cross is well strated in this picture of the down 'Flying Scotsman' ading out of the terminus hauled by Deltic No. 55011 *The yal Northumberland Fusiliers* which was allocated to teshead depot at Newcastle for all its working days, cept for a short period at York before withdrawal. The ture was taken from above Gas Works Tunnel on 10th July 76. In the background is St. Pancras Station roof, and the ver of the hotel, with the refuelling shed in the locomotive d on the right hand side. – *Gavin Morrison*

PUBLISHED BY

ATLANTIC TRANSPORT PUBLISHERS
TREVITHICK HOUSE · WEST END · PENRYN
CORNWALL TR10 8HE · ENGLAND

AUTHOR'S INTRODUCTION

ALWAYS regarded as the principal high-speed route in the country, the East Coast Main Line has probably undergone more changes than any other comparable part of our railway network in the approximate 30-year period covered by this volume. Most of these changes have been in consequence of the commercial need to keep the competitive edge which high-speed rail transit offers compared with its road (and even, at times, airline) competition.

To put this into some sort of historical perspective, one has only to note that in the comparable 1930-1960 period, far fewer basic changes took place. The 1930s started with the original Gresley pacifics in charge and they were still there some 30 years later, albeit augmented by later designs, mostly from the same stable. Neither did long-distance trains change too much in basic principle. Gresley corridor coaches (plus Thompson and BR Mk1 successors after c.1950) held sway and operating procedures hardly changed at all.

By contrast, the 1960s began with a flourish in the form of the celebrated Deltics in full squadron service from 1962, along with the first regular 100 mph trains and extensive re-signalling and track re-alignment to cope with them. During this time, the expresses themselves gradually changed from Mk1 plus a few late pre-BR survivors to the fully air-conditioned Mk2 vehicles, which were not long in full operation before the line was extensively re-equipped again with the celebrated 125 mph HSTs and Mk3 coaches from 1978. Not much more than ten years later, these trains too were replaced by the 140 mph Class 91 electrics and Mk4 stock – and I have not even mentioned the similar changes in both the short distance passenger and freight operating fields.

At the more superficial level, there were no fewer than three basic changes of livery during the same period, along with several minor variations. The 1960s started with the old 'steam age' colour schemes still in evidence but in 1965, the corporate image blue and grey liveries gradually began to take over on all stock. These too are now mostly history, having been replaced on the main line from the mid 1980s by the (current) InterCity livery, augmented by several other sector colour schemes for more local traff[ic] depending on where one might be.

I have been fortunate to have been able to photograph most [of] the changes myself (often with the active support of BR offici[als] too numerous to name but to whom I would like to express [my] sincere thanks), and in this book I have tried to present the m[ost] interesting of these things I have been able to record. In so[me] cases, I have had to use images from other photographers to [get] the mixture I wanted and to these several gentlemen (who[se] names are acknowledged alongside their pictures) I would like [to] offer my sincere thanks.

I have adopted a fairly conventional approach in terms of p[re]sentation – in effect, a 'journey' northwards from King's Cros[s] and along the way, I hope I have managed to show that the [so]called modern railway can offer just as much variety to t[he] observant onlooker as did its predecessor. G.W.[

BELOW, LEFT: The everyday sight inside Kings Cross in 1990. A Driving Van Trailer (DVT) at the head of a rake of Mk 4 coaches with [a] Class 91 electric at the north end, is ready to depart for Leeds. Alongside is Class 43 HST power car No. 43038, in its unique all yell[ow] front end livery, having arrived with the 07.30 Pullman from Leeds o[n] 15th March. Gavin Morris[on]

BELOW: A dirty looking Cravens DMU, leaves the terminus with a tra[in] for the outer suburbs on 10th July 1976. These units when new were allocated to Finsbury Park although they went to Cambridge for maintenance. Rolls Royce DMUs also came to the Great Northern suburban services after the Lea Valley line was electrified, and were maintained by Stratford. They worked to Moorgate as locomotive hauled trains were not allowed due to length problems; but the locomotives could work to Broad Street.

The appearance of this unit is in marked contrast to the striking livery of the present day Network South East Units. Gavin Morris[on]

BELOW: On the wet Sunday morning of 7th March 1976, four Deltics are present in the yard at Kings Cross. Inside the shed is No.. 55012 *Crepello,* with 55003 *Meld* and 55021 *Argyll and Sutherland Highlander* outside, and No. 55010 *The King's Own Scottish Borderer* just visible in the background. The yard was primarily used for re-fuelling and became very congested at times. After the High Speed Trains took over the services, it was closed in May 1979, and currently presents a very unattractive sight as one enters Kings Cross   Gavin Morrison

RIGHT: Class 31 No. D5650, later to become No. 31224, and showing its 34G shedplate, pauses at Wood Green whilst working an up suburban train on 17th August 1967.   John Glover

BELOW, RIGHT: Finsbury Park depot opened in April 1960 as a new purpose built diesel depot and provided the motive power for trains out of Kings Cross. It was the home of the famous Deltic 'racehorses' for virtually all their working days where they were maintained by enthusiastic staff, and kept in excellent mechanical as well as external condition. No. 55015 *Tulyar* is inside on 2nd April 1981, sporting the white cab which was the special feature of the Finsbury Park fleet. The plaque on the nose of the locomotive was to commerate the locomotive attending the celebrations at Rainhill in May 1980. The depot buildings were demolished towards the end of 1991 and the site cleared.   Gavin Morrison

3

ABOVE: Before the introduction of the Mk 4 coaches and the purpose-built DVTs, the Class 91 electrics started running between Kings Cross and Leeds using HST Mk 3 stock, with modified Class 43 (HST) power units, acting as surrogate DVTs. The combined power of the Class 91 and HST power car produced some incredible acceleration away from stations, giving excellent opportunities to record the performances with the stop watch. An unidentified Class 91 is seen heading North past Hadley Wood with the 16.25 departure from Kings Cross on the 18th May 1989.

J. S. White

RIGHT: Looking extremely smart in the Network South East livery, Class 313 EMU No. 313058 emerges from the tunnel at Hadley Wood, whilst working a Welwyn to Moorgate service in August 1990.

L. A. Nixon

BELOW: Evening commuters are rushed home at 90mph by a Class 312 EMU as it heads north between the tunnels at Hadley Wood to the north of the station on 19th September 1980. The outer suburban services were electrified on 6th February 1978 and the Class 312s have now been replaced by the Class 317s.

Gavin Morrison

LEFT: A very impressive view of Welwyn Viad[uct]
also known as Digswell viaduct. It is 1490ft lo[ng]
and 89ft high, built of brick with 40 arches ea[ch]
of 30ft span, and is a lasting memorial to the
famous railway contractor T. Brassey. On 13t[h]
June 1962 the down 'Master Cutler' Pullman i[s]
seen crossing hauled by the Brush prototype
D0280 Falcon, painted in a smart green livery. [It]
entered service at Finsbury Park in October 1[9..]
and was fitted with two Bristol-Siddeley MD 6[..]
engines, as fitted to the Class 52 'Westerns'. [It]
was sold to British Rail in January 1971 and
became Class 53 and numbered D1200. It the[n]
spent most of its time allocated to Ebbw
Junction until withdrawn in October 1975.

Cliff Woodhead

BELOW: Twenty-eight years separate the
pictures on this page, both taken on Welwyn
viaduct. In 1962 it was the early days of the m[ain]
line diesels on the route; by 1990 the Class 91
electrics were in use on the Leeds trains, as i[s]
shown in the picture taken on 1st August 199[0]

L. A. Nixon

1985, the Class 317 EMUs were introduced on the East Coast mainline working to Peterborough and Cambridge, allowing the Class 312s to be cascaded to the Great Eastern lines. In this view, No. 317348, working a Royston-Kings Cross service, leaves Welwyn in August 1990. These 100mph units have given an excellent account of themselves on the Great Northern suburban services.   L. A. Nixon

ABOVE: A view of Peterborough looking south from the road bridge to the north of the station before the electrification masts were installed. On the 16th October 1976 Class 47 No. 47079 *George Jackson Churchward,* which is hardly appropriate for Peterborough, is leaving with a northbound tank train. In the background, Deltic No. 55001 *St. Paddy* prepares to leave with a down Kings Cross-Leeds express.   Gavin Morrison

LEFT: The first English Electric Type 4 to work on the east coast main line was D201 which was allocated to Hornsey depot, and one of its regular duties was the 'Master Cutler' Pullman train to Sheffield. The locomotive later became No. 40001 and lasted until July 1984. It is seen in its heyday on the 21st June 1960 heading the up Pullman past Werrington Junction.
                    Dennis Ovenden

Class 40 No. 40111 bursts out of Stoke Tunnel into the sunshine, heading the 12.04 Kings Cross to Hull express on 27th May 1978. The locomotive was allocated to the LM Region at the time, but on summer Saturdays, Type 4 locomotives from all over turned up. Stoke Tunnel is 880 yards long and 101 miles from Kings Cross, just north of the summit of the 20 miles of climbing up Stoke Bank from Werrington, where the water troughs were once located. Gavin Morrison

THROUGH THE YEARS AT LITTLE PONTON

ABOVE LEFT: The Deltic prototype storming up the climb to Stoke Tunnel on 5th September 1959, working an up express from Doncaster to Kings Cross.
Gavin Morrison

ABOVE: Deltic No. D9018 *Ballymoss* in original two-tone green livery before the addition of the yellow nose panel, heading the up 'Flying Scotsman' on 7th July 1962.
Gavin Morrison

LEFT: The 15-40 Leeds to Kings Cross headed by Class 47 No. 47507, which became Class 47/7 No. 47716 *Duke of Edinburgh's Award* now in the Network South East fleet, heads south on 27th May 1978.

Gavin Morrison

Obviously, there was a shortage of Type 4 motive power at Kings Cross, as Class 31s
Nos. 31153 and 31231 had been pressed into service on the morning Kings Cross to
Scarborough on 27th May 1978. They were slightly down on schedule and had hardly
got out of sight before Deltic No. 55016 *Gordon Highlander* emerged from the 968 yards
Peascliffe Tunnel on the 09-00 Kings Cross-Edinburgh.   Gavin Morrison

LEFT: Seen from above Peascliffe Tunnel, Deltic No. 55002 *The King's Own Yorkshire Light Infantry,* is storming south at a speed in the upper 90s hauling the 08.30 Leeds-Kings Cross on 27th May 1978. The Napier engines could be heard well before it had got to Barkston Junction, which can just be seen at the end of the avenue of trees. This locomotive is now in the National Railway Museum at York, and is in working order.

Gavin Morrison

ABOVE: The 100mph restriction sign is clearly displayed in this picture of an up HST for Kings Cross passing over the diamond crossing just north of Newark Station, in September 1981. Just visible in the background is the girder bridge taking the tracks across the River Trent.

L. A. Nixon

RIGHT: Class 47 No. 47217 heads north past Tuxford on a returning Rugby Cup Final special from London on 2nd May 1982. Just to the right of the locomotive here was a junction with the ex-Great Central line, which crossed over the ECML about one mile further south. Tuxford once had a busy goods yard, and a locomotive depot, to work local coal traffic from the Nottinghamshire Coal Field and other trains through to Lincoln.

Gavin Morrison

LEFT: In wintry conditions, a brand new HST set No. 254006, heads south at Rossington on a driver training duty on 10th February 1978. It is at Rossington, five miles south of Doncaster, that the merry-go-round traffic from the Yorkshire Coal Field starts to use the East Coast main line.

Gavin Morrison

RIGHT: Up to the end of the 1970s, Black Carr Junction, about three miles south of Doncaster Station where the Lincoln line joins, used to have a fine selection of signal gantries. On 6th July 1977 the down loop line was already out of use, as is seen in the picture of Class 47 No. 47407, later named *Aycliffe,* heading the 13.00 express from Kings Cross to Edinburgh.

Gavin Morrison

ABOVE: The extensive sidings for Merry-go-Round traffic are show in this picture of Black Carr, not long before the electrification masts were erected. In the foreground Class 56 No. 56125 heads for the yard to the other side of the ring road bridge, whilst in the background, No. 56017 just out of Doncaster Works in the then new Railfreight grey livery, prepares to head south. The picture was taken on 17th September 1985.

Gavin Morrison

BELOW: The current depot at Doncaster known as Carr Loco is on the site of the former large steam shed, coded 36A. It has never had an allocation of main line diesels, but is always very busy doing minor exams and fuelling locomotives for the many freight activities in the area. It also has tyre turning facilities, and, of course, is used for dealing with locomotives awaiting a visit to the works and after they have been repaired. Three Class 47s, Nos. 47301, 47238 and 47836, all in different sector liveries, await a visit to the works. In the background is the new control centre for the electrified main line, which will control the section from Stoke in the south to Belford in the north.

Gavin Morrison

...ridge Junction just south of Doncaster Station ...as a splendid vantage point in both directions ...o observe and photograph the trains until the ...ectrification masts and wires were installed. ...eltic No. 55015 *Tulyar* had been given the special beauty treatment by Finsbury Park Depot for a ceremony to commemorate its participation in the Rainhill festivities. The ceremony had taken place in the morning at the depot, when the plaque visible on the nose was unveiled. The date was 17th March 1981, and it then worked the 12.20 Kings Cross to York. It is travelling on the down slow line, as the main tracks were being realigned to raise the speed limit for the HSTs.   Gavin Morrison

LEFT: The view looking north at Bridge Junction on 27th June 1986, as Inverness allocated Class 47 No. 47460 heads south on the 'Venice Simplon Orient Express.' In the loop on the left is a failed HST, about to be rescued by a Class 56 locomotive. After waiting for about 45 minutes on a hot evening, many of the passengers who were leaving the train at Doncaster got fed up, left the train and finished the journey on foot down the main road!

Gavin Morrison

ABOVE: A group of locomotives outside the 'Plant' at Doncaster awaiting both entry to works and return to traffic on 28th March 1986. From left to right, Class 31 No. 31229 is ex-works, No. 31240 has fire damage, No. 03179 is in the background, Class 50 No. 50005 *Collingwood* is ex-works, Class 56 No. 56112 awaits works attention, and No. 56098 is seen passing on the Sheffield line.

Gavin Morrison

BELOW: To commemorate the 50th anniversary of Gresley's A4 Pacific *Mallard's* world speed record run of 126mph on 3rd July 1938 down Stoke Bank, British Rail really rose to the occasion with an immaculately turned out train from Kings Cross, hauled to Doncaster by the unique Class 89 electric locomotive No. 89001, later named *Avocet*. *Mallard* took over at Doncaster for a trip to Scarborough, and the area on and around the station has probably never seen such crowds. The Class 89 worked the train back to Kings Cross, and is seen in the evening sun as it passes Bridge Junction.

Gavin Morrison

19

LEFT: The Class 50 locomotives have never worked regularly on the East Coast main line, except on test trains after overhaul at Doncaster Works to Newcastle and Peterborough. The extremely grubby redundant coaches used on the test trains were in marked contrast to the immaculate ex-works locomotives. Many hours have been spent by enthusiasts over the years to try and capture the Class 50s on their test train outings, and on the 16th May 1986 it was the turn of No. 50036 *Victorious* to have a trip to Peterborough. It is seen in the sidings to the south of the station, before reversing the stock into the station and heading south. In the background can be seen the works or the 'Plant' as it is known.

Gavin Morrison

ABOVE: Selby was an interesting centre, with so many lines converging on the station, plus the swing bridge, and in the past a steam depot. The signal box at the north end of the down platform was out of use when this picture was taken on the 2nd September 1983. A down HST is heading over the bridge, which was opened in 1891, the main span being 130ft. long.

Gavin Morrison

BELOW: Seen from the top of the Selby Swing Bridge, Class 31 No. 31320 heads north on a permanent way train. Notice that it has passed over the down centre road through the station; these centre roads were removed after the line to York was abandoned. There is a speed limit of 40mph over the bridge, which had always been a nuisance to non-stop trains.

Gavin Morrison

ABOVE: A very lucky picture taken at Bishop's Wood on the Selby avoiding line on 27th December, 1991. An up HST with loco No. 43049 *Neville Hill* meets Class 91 No. 91031 *Sir Henry Royce* closing on each other at around 250 mph as they race north and south. The new line was constructed between Colton Junction in the north and Temple Hirst Junction in the south.
Gavin Morrison

RIGHT: The construction of the York by-pass, running to the south of the city, not only helped the traffic congestion, but created a splendid vantage point to photograph the up trains powering away from Chaloner's Whin Junction. On Sunday 10th October 197 the 11.00 Edinburgh-Kings Cross was photographed at this location hauled by Haymarket Deltic No. 55019 *Royal Highland Fusilier,* which has been preserved by the Deltic Preservation Society, and is currently in full working order. At around this time t locomotive could be distinguished from the other Deltics as it was the only one carryin two numbers on each side.
Gavin Morriso

ABOVE: A perfectly timed picture at Chalone Whin Junction shows Deltic No. 55014 *The Duke of Wellington's Regiment* rounding the curve at speed on the down 'Talisman', 16.0 Kings Cross-Edinburgh, just as a double headed empty ore train headed by Class 37s Nos. 37042 and 37164 (now 37676) cross ov to the down slow line on 2nd June 1977.

Gavin Morris

BELOW: A panoramic view of the now close Dringhouses Yard, which was situated abou 1½ miles south of York Station on the up-sid The 12.40 from Edinburgh to Kings Cross, headed by Haymarket Deltic No. 55004 *Queen's Own Highlander,* passes an unidentified Class 37 and Class 08 shunter. 55004 spent a short spell at the end of its career based at York, from where it was withdrawn in November 1981.

Gavin Morris

RIGHT: This impressive picture, taken from footbridge above where the racecourse stati used to be, shows Class 31 No. 31253 (later become No. 31431) heading south under Holgate Bridge, just as an unidentified Class 40 heads north. This bridge presented quite few problems when it came to electrifying th railway and had to be raised to give adequat clearances. The date of the picture was 2nd September 1975.

Gavin Morris

LEFT: The north end of old platform 9 at York (now platform 5) has been a favourite location for photographers for many years. A down HST in original livery pauses under the super station roof which is 81ft. high, on its journey north on 12th October 1980.   J. S. Whiteley

OPPOSITE: The 26th May 1978 sees a double-headed Class 37 down tank train, with locomotives Nos. 37079 (now No. 37357) and 37007 (now 37506) approaching Clifton at the north end of York, having taken the avoiding line. In the background can be seen the York Carriage and Wagon Works, which have now become part of British Rail Engineering Ltd. (BREL), where many of the recent EMU classes have been built.

Gavin Morrison

RIGHT: A unique event occurred at York Station in the early morning of Sunday 19th March 1978, when a line-up was organised representing the express motive power that had worked expresses on the East Coast Main Line over the years. The complete line-up consisted of the Stirling Single No. 1, North Eastern 4-4-0 No. 1621, Great Northern large boilered Atlantic No. 251, A4 Pacific No. 4468 *Mallard,* Deltic No. 55013 *The Black Watch* and HST set No. 254009. By about 10.30 am all the exhibits had been removed. The reason for the event was special filming.

Gavin Morrison

BELOW: Recently ex-works on 5th April 1978, English Electric Class 40 No. 40155 passed non-stop through the north end of Clifton yard at York with a cement train for Clitheroe.   Gavin Morrison

RIGHT: An immaculate Class 47 No. 47321 heads a northbound freight down the fast line just south of Pilmoor, 16 miles north of York on the East Coast 'race' track between York and Darlington. In the background on the right can be seen a signal box which is where the line to Malton via Ampleforth used to leave the main line at Sunbeck Junction East, and provided a direct route from the north to Scarborough. To the right of the signal box there used to be several signals without any track to control and which were used for driver eyesight tests.

Gavin Morrison

TOP: A remarkable sight near Sessay on 22nd August 1975 of a very dirty unidentified Class 47 rapidly overtaking Great Northern Atlantic No. 990 *Henry Oakley,* hauling the famous Stirling Single No. 1 from the National Railway Museum to Shildon to take part in the 150 years celebrations of the opening of the Stockton and Darlington railway.

Gavin Morrison

CENTRE: Class 47 No. 47552 opens up past Northallerton after a signal check on its way north with a down express on 26th August 1975, and passes preserved Modified Hall No. 6960 *Raveningham Hall,* dumped in the yard after failing en route to the Stockton and Darlington 150 celebrations.

Gavin Morrison

BOTTOM: One of the Darlington batch of Class 25s No. 25024, built in March 1962 and withdrawn in January 1976, heads south with an up-freight under one of many modern bridges crossing the line north of York on 26th August 1975.

Gavin Morrison

RIGHT: Passing the site of the old Stockton and Darlington crossing, a complete Trans-Pennine coach set, headed by the unique liveried Class 47 No. 47475 approaches Darlington with the 16.20 service from Newcastle to Liverpool on 11th July 1989.

P. J. Robinson

LEFT: The Eastgate to Tyne Yard cement train leaves Darlington after reversing on the evening of 10th May 1988, headed by Thornaby based Class 37 No. 37074.

P. J. Robinson

ABOVE: An immaculate Class 47 No. 47637 *Springburn* in Scotrail Intercity livery heads the 12.43 Newcastle-Plymouth mail train at Childon near Ferryhill. This locomotive has now lost its nameplate and is numbered 47826. The date was 16th February 1988.

P. J. Robinson

RIGHT: Taking it easy on the speed restricted curves at Sunderland Bridge just north of Croxdale, a well-turned-out Haymarket Deltic No. 55019 *Royal Highland Fusilier,* heads north on 30th May 1978 with the 09.00 Kings Cross-Edinburgh.

Gavin Morrison

LEFT: Train 5V01, the 17.34 Heaton to York Postal empties, is hauled south by Class 31 No. 31428 *The North Yorkshire Moors Railw* on 3rd May 1990. As can be seen the electrification masts and wires are now in position at Stonebridge. Relly Mill Junction used to be just north of this location where lines from Consett, Bishop Auckland and Waterhouses used to join the main line.

P. J. Robins

BELOW: This very different view from the same location at Stonebridge, approximatel 2 miles south of Durham, was taken from th bridge which is shown in the view above. Th 18.00 Newcastle-Liverpool Trans-Pennine service, hauled by Class 45 No. 45010, hea south on 30th May 1978.

Gavin Morris

ABOVE: Plawsworth Viaduct to the south of Chester-le-Street is the setting for this picture of an unidentified Class 46 heading south in the evening light on 4th September 1975.   Gavin Morrison

RIGHT: High above Chester-le-Street town centre, Class 47 No. 47524 heads south on 28th September 1975 over the viaduct with an up-express.
                                                                                              Gavin Morrison

LEFT: A lucky picture on 11th May 1979 at Tyne Yard showing Class 40 No. 40002, which was a Healey Mills locomotive at the time, arriving with a permanent way train, just as the 15.00 from Kings Cross to Edinburgh passes with Deltic No. 55006 *The Fife and Forfar Yeomanary* in charge.

P. J. Robinson

ABOVE: An immaculate coal sector Class 56 No. 56125 rounds the well-known bend off the King Edward Bridge at Gateshead, working the colourful 6M21 9.55 West Blyth to Ellesmere Port Cawoods coal train on 22nd June 1988.

P. J. Robinson

LEFT: One of the Class 142 'Pacer' units No. 142025, displaced from Devon and Cornwall due to being unsuitable for the branch lines in the area, is leaving Newcastle on 20th June 1990, working the 10.23 to Berwick. The transfer of these units to Newcastle, Leeds and Manchester helped to cover for the very poor availability of the Class 143s and 142s in these areas.

P. J. Robinson

RIGHT, TOP: Gateshead-allocated Deltic No. 55017 The *Durham Light Infantry*, at the head of the 08.00 Edinburgh Waverley to Kings Cross on 17th August 1977 passing Pegswood, about 2 miles north of Morpeth. In the background is the site of a former colliery together with the cottages and spoil heap. Currently the site is now a modern housing estate, with trees covering the mound.

Gavin Morrison

RIGHT, BELOW: In the days when the Kings Cross-Edinburgh trains were 12 coaches, Finsbury Park Deltic No. D9020 *Nimbus,* in the original two-tone green livery but with yellow nose panel, approaches Alnmouth just before the bottom of the climb at 1 in 170 to Little Mill. The date was 21st May 1966. This locomotive was the first of the Class, together with *St. Paddy,* to be withdrawn in December 1979.

Gavin Morrison

BELOW: The Royal Border Bridge over the River Tweed at Berwick is undoubtedly the most impressive structure on the East Coast main line, and unlike so many other fine viaducts, it is possible to obtain an uninterrupted view of it. It cost £120,000 to build, it is 2,160ft. long, 126½ft. high at the highest point and has 28 arches, each of 61ft. 6in. diameter.

Deltic No. 55022 *Royal Scots Grey* passes over on the down 14.00 Kings Cross-Edinburgh on 28th June 1976. In the background is Tweedmouth, where the steam locomotive depot used to be situated, which served the border branches as well as the main line.

Gavin Morrison

RIGHT: In the days when there was plenty of freight traffic using the line between Newcastle and Edinburgh, the loops at Berwick were well used to let the expresses overtake. The 14.00 from Kings Cross has just passed, so Class 26 No. 26006 sets off on the climb to Grantshouse, 16 miles further north, where it can, if necessary, be looped again. The date was 28th June 1976.

Gavin Morrison

LEFT: In the mid-1970s and early 1980s, the 17.10 from Edinburgh to Berwick evening commuter train was worked by a wide variety of motive power. It then returned empty stock back to the Scottish capital. On 28th June 1976 an immaculate Class 25 No. 25226 was in charge, and is shown travelling along the clifftops above the North Sea, south of Burnmouth.

Gavin Morrison

BELOW: Just south of the site of Burnmouth Station, where the line turns inland towards Ayton and Reston, there is this superb location with the sea in the background. On 2nd June 1978 the clear evening light picks out Deltic No. 55017 *The Durham Light Infantry,* heading south with the 17.00 from Edinburgh Waverley to Kings Cross. The branch to Eyemouth left the main line about one mile north of Burnmouth Station, and closed to traffic on 5th February 1962.

Gavin Morrison

BELOW: Sweeping round the speed restricted curves at Houndwood, Class 40 No. 40182 in ex-works condition, heads north on the 29th July 1978 with the through Liverpool-Edinburgh, which the locomotive would have worked throughout. It is about to cross one of the many bridges that were replaced after the disastrous floods in this area in 1948.

Gavin Morrison

RIGHT: The locomotive and the surroundings make a very colourful picture at Penmansheil as Class 37 No. 37518 heads the 7X50 British Steel Corporation Train from Hartlepool to Leith on 17th June 1987. The hill in the left-hand background was the one through which the line used to travel before its disastrous collapse in April 1979. The line had to be completely re-aligned, avoiding the hill, and it was not re-opened until August.

P. J. Robinson

LEFT, TOP: The Torness Nuclear Power Station dominates the skyline as an HST, forming the 13.35 Edinburgh-Kings Cross passes on the 16th September 1987, powered by units Nos. 43113 and 43062.
Gavin Morrison

LEFT, BOTTOM: A view taken from the now disused down platform at Dunbar, showing the 11.35 from Kings Cross to Edinburgh arriving on 16th September 1987. The through lines can be seen on the right. The HST is running in a somewhat unusual nine car formation between the power cars instead of the usual eight.
Gavin Morrison

OPPOSITE, TOP LEFT: Railfreight liveried Class 26 on electrification duties at Cockenzie on 20th March 1989.
L. A. Nixon

OPPOSITE, TOP RIGHT: Deltic No. 55011 *The Royal Northumberland Fusiliers,* just ex works, accelerates past Portobello junction on the 12.10 Aberdeen-Kings Cross on 3rd June 1978. The junction in the left background is the old Waverley route, and the now closed freightliner terminal can be seen on the far right-hand side.
Gavin Morrison

OPPOSITE, BOTTOM LEFT: The 10.00 Aberdeen-Kings Cross HST headed by No. 43116 on 16th September 1987, passes Portobello with the closed freightliner depot in the background.
Gavin Morrison

OPPOSITE, BOTTOM RIGHT: Deltic No. 55007 *Pinza* emerges from Carlton Tunnel into Edinburgh Waverley, with a Dunbar shuttle service during the closure of the East Coast Main Line in 1979 due to the Penmansheil Tunnel collapse.
Gavin Morrison

LEFT: Inside Edinburgh Waverley Station, Scotrail Class 47 No. 47461 *Charles Rennie Mackintosh,* prepares to head the 11.42 to Inverness from Platform 11 on 19th April 1990.

J. S. Whiteley

BELOW: No book on the east coast mine line would be complete without reference to Haymarket Depot, in steam days coded 64B. The condition in which it kept its steam locomotives in the 1950s is legendary, as well as its diesels thereafter. This everyday line-up taken on 3 June 1978, shows Class 47 No. 47268 (now 47595), Deltic No. 55018 *Ballymoss* and Class 40 No. 40142 ready for their next duties. This is now all history as the depot entered a new era in 1990 taking over the maintenance of the Class 158 fleet allocated to Scotland as well as the other Scotrail Sprinters.

Gavin Morrison